Emilio Robba

The Art of Arranging Silk Flowers

Emilio Robba

The Art of Arranging Silk Flowers

Text by Mimi Luebbermann
Photographs by Louis Gaillard

William Morrow and Company, Inc. New York

Library of Congress Cataloging-in-Publication Data

Robba, Emilio.
    The art of arranging silk flowers / Emilio Robba ; text by Mimi
Luebbermann ; photographs by Louis Gaillard.
        p.   cm.
    Includes index.
    ISBN 0-688-14840-9
    1. Silk flowers. 2. Flower arrangement.   I. Luebbermann, Mimi.
II. Title.
TT890.7.R63   1998
745.92—dc21   97-31781
                                                              CIP

Printed in the United States of America

First Edition

2 3 4 5 6 7 8 9 10

BOOK DESIGN BY JOEL AVIROM
DESIGN ASSISTANTS: JASON SNYDER AND MEGHAN DAY HEALEY

www.williammorrow.com

Ma mère et mon père

CONTENTS

The Eternal Ephemeral   *9*

Introduction   *13*

PART ONE

The Natural Approach to Design   *19*

PART TWO

The Art of Arrangements   *53*

PART THREE

The Seasonal Approach   *85*

PART FOUR

Tools and Materials   *115*

List of Ingredients for Bouquets   *125*

Acknowledgments   *126*

Sources   *126*

Index   *127*

THE ETERNAL EPHEMERAL

I have always felt that nature would guide all aspects of my life. I remember how moved I was when as a small child I first watched my mother arrange a simple bouquet of flowers in a brilliant array of colors. Later, when I studied at the Beaux-Arts School, I was exhilarated when shapes and colors recalled for me the outlines of flowers, and the hues of forest and meadow. When I joined my sister and brother at our first flower shop thirty years ago, the fragrant air, the patterns and tones of flowers—from piney greens and blooming bulbs to bright autumn leaves—mesmerized me. I knew flowers were my world, and I've been fortunate to be able to live in that world ever since.

When we started out we had little money, so I began to fill my fresh flower arrangements with materials from the wild. I gathered moss, rocks, crooked branches, and grasses from the forests and fields. In 1978, these "moss gardens" became a sensation in Paris, and inspired a new style of floral arranging.

My work continued to flow organically from there. In the early 1980s, I was asked to organize an exhibit of thousands of precious orchids at the Musée d'Histoire Naturelle in Paris. The show brought me great recognition, and consequently, Pierre Cardin asked me to create a retail store that would sell the finest flowers, including many unusual species, under the prestigious "Maxim's de Paris" label. For many years, I provided the flowers for the President of the French Republic's airplane. During that time the press baptized me "Sculptor of flowers." I have indeed been blessed.

A few flowers combined with natural elements create a miniature moss garden.

Though I had worked with flowers for many years, in the course of my travels I discovered that there was still much more to learn. In Japan I discovered ikebana, their traditional floral art. Though I was born in Paris, I was raised by my Italian parents in a wonderfully effusive Latin culture; therefore, the "minimalist" rigor of ikebana seemed distant from my roots. But ikebana proved to be a great revelation to me. It taught me to understand the intricate designs and structure of the natural world. Ikebana taught me how to build, how to determine the need for balance as well as for asymmetry, and how to make an arrangement simple with the use of fine techniques. It seems paradoxical, but the more beautiful the results of any creation, the less obvious the hard work that went into the making of it. In ikebana, I learned the discipline of arranging flowers so that only the purity and the magic remain.

In the early 1990s, I began to move in a new direction, a direction that, given my love of nature, I could never have anticipated. Thanks to my many journeys to Asia, I discovered that there were fabric flowers—newly designed—with surprisingly natural qualities. My preconception of these flowers—often wrongfully called "artificial"—as inadequate was replaced with astonishment first, and then with attraction and admiration. What I witnessed was a true transformation, afforded by new materials and modern techniques (both technological and handcrafted), which yielded fabric flowers that truly recover the delicacy and fragility of the first flowers created by the Chinese centuries ago. This new generation of silk flowers is so lifelike (the silky transparency of their petals, the veins in their foliage filled with sap, and the bloom of their spring buds) that they can actually fill the same need we have in our lives for fresh flowers. A veritable painter's palette, the rainbow of fabric colors available—from shockingly bright to delicate pastel, dazzlingly new or old-fashioned—is magnificent and seemingly infinite.

The possibility of remaking nature, which is so complex and so vulnerable, bothered me for many years. I feared losing the spirit of the organic, with its imperfections.

But all that has changed for me in the act of creativity that can be achieved with arranging fabric flowers. I taught myself to play with the shapes of flowers and foliage to realize natural creations, where the subtle plays off against the spectacular.

Nature is said to be perfect, but it is the imperfection that touches me most. When you arrange flowers, do not try to make every arrangement perfect; give freedom to your design. Enjoy nature's imperfections with a bit of off-kilter balance, or a flower whose stem crinkles, or blossoms with petals just dropping off, and your works will be all the more natural for their slight irregularities.

I wrote this book to share with you my lifelong pleasure in sculpting with flowers. The pages of *The Art of Arranging Silk Flowers* will guide you to your own choices, while keeping you out of bad marriages of shapes and colors. Everyone is talented enough to work with silk flowers; a few basic guidelines on pattern, color, form, and technique will get you started. Flowers can speak in many languages. You can design arrangements based on your mood, whether it's classical, modern, rustic, or romantic. In this book you will learn three different techniques: flowers arranged in the illusion of water, florist's foam block, and hand-held bouquets. You'll learn to extend the natural-versus-artifical paradox by mixing fabric flowers with preserved foliage. You can plan arrangements in tune with nature by designing seasonal bouquets—or remain in an everlasting summer. You can even marry fabric flowers to outdoor bushes, blending real and artificial flowers outside in your garden. *The Art of Arranging Silk Flowers* will show you how to enliven your arrangements by working on each leaf and each flower, petal by petal.

Follow me on a journey to the land of the "eternal ephemeral," where you can fullfil your dream of filling your life with luminous, beautiful flowers that last forever.

— EMILIO ROBBA

Iceland poppy bud
and bloom

*The Eternal
Ephemeral*

11

INTRODUCTION

$\mathcal{I}$magine your home radiant with flowers—all the time. Every morning you would wake to find glorious pink peonies on your bedside table or brightly colored dahlias on the kitchen counter. With the new generation of fine silk flowers, this fantasy need no longer remain just a dream. Today's silk flowers are as beautiful as the real thing—and they can last a lifetime with a minimum of care: their petals don't wither, the stems don't mold, and their beauty remains constant. Because they are drawn more closely from nature than ever before, silk flowers are wonderfully lifelike; each fabric petal or stem is superbly detailed—veins and spots make their way through leaves and petals, and light shines brilliantly through the translucent fabric.

With this new availability of lifelike flowers, arranging them can now become a regular source of pleasure in your life. In the past, flower arranging was dictated by strict formulas that limited personal taste and style. Now you can throw away the rules. Using these extraordinarily natural arrangements as your guide, you can proceed with confidence to develop your own design instincts. You will learn how to evaluate your home for the kinds of arrangements that will work with the particular color, light, and space available. You will learn about harmony, height, and texture, and how each plays a special role in the process. Whether you follow the step-by-step recipes pictured in these pages, or just absorb the ideas and beautifully photographed arrangements, you will learn to make gracious floral sculptures a natural part of your life.

Natural light will always enhance a silk flower arrangement.

History

    *A*rchaeologists, searching the tombs of ancient Egypt, have uncovered painted lotus flowers created from linen, the earliest permanent flowers. In ancient China, flowers were fashioned from the thinnest slivers of wood and tinted with colored dust long before they were sewn from silk. Thoughout the ages, flowers have been crafted from fabric, glass, wax, feathers, and beads, as well as painted on canvases and fashioned into jewelry from bright, sparkling gems. Humankind has long tried to preserve and copy the flower.

    In 1738, the French chemist and botanist, Seguin de Mende-en-Gévaudan began the first large-scale manufacture of silk flowers in Paris. Tinting the leaves with silver, he made both table decorations and flowers for women's clothing. In a grand gesture, he created gardens from these flowers; he draped trellises in cleverly fashioned cloth roses, and covered trees with fabric fruit and flowers.

    In America in the nineteenth century, cloth flowers were crafted by workers who cut out petals and leaves using specially designed cutting irons and tweezers, never touching the flowers with their fingers. The term "artificial flower" originated in the early twentieth century when awkward, stalky imitations with bright green rubber stems, often incorrectly colored, were touted as fine reproductions. With the discovery of plastic, the artificial flower industry began to improve its product. It wasn't until the late 1960s that manufacturers experimented with polyester fabrics and plastic-covered wire to make flowers that actually resembled their natural counterparts. Although silk fabric is rarely used in production today, most of the flowers are still labeled "silk," evoking their early beginnings.

Silk flowers of foxglove and sweet pea are interplanted in an outdoor garden.

Manufacturing Today:
The New Generation of Silk Flowers

*T*he top-quality flowers made today are produced in Asia, where they are designed with exquisite botanical accuracy. Shaped from professionally sculpted molds, they are superior in every way to the earlier fabric flowers. Although they are still called "silk," the individual flower parts are actually cut from synthetic fibers. The fabric is pressed over heated molds that melt the plastic fibers to retain the subtle shape and character of individual flowers, producing the particular arch of a magnolia petal or the splayed rays of a sunflower. Painters working from photographs then brush on gradations of color, so each part—from stems to leaves to blossoms—mimics the real plant.

One painter tints the edges of the petals of the lady's slipper orchid and another adds striated color lines radiating out from the pouch. Stems or the undersides of leaves are surfaced and colored with thorns, bumps, or special textures. After all the parts are formed and painted, they are then assembled, piece by piece. Some flowers require sixty steps of painting, shaping, and combining to capture their full natural beauty. The flowers are then carefully packed to preserve their individual characteristics through the long shipping journey.

With advice and encouragement from designers around the world, the fabric flower industry continues to expand its repertoire to include fruits, vegetables, nuts, berries, and more unusual flowers and plants. The new collections meet the passions of today's gardeners, providing everything from herbs to heirloom flowers.

OPPOSITE:
A lady's slipper orchid, with fine hairs along the edges of the petals, displays the realistic detail of today's silk flowers.

LEFT:
A magnolia blossom has subtly shaded petals; its leaves are flocked with a light tan texture on the underside.

PART ONE

—

The Natural Approach to Design

To design natural-looking fabric-flower arrangements, turn to nature, which is always the best teacher. When you begin to notice how leaves twist and turn to the sun, how flower buds swell to bursting, and how petals gradually unfurl, you develop an instinctive sense of how to design. One of the wonderful aspects of working with silk flowers is how it helps you notice the natural world more keenly. When you walk down the street you suddenly realize how an iris opens in a sidewalk garden, or you find yourself visiting the florist more often to take a peek at how the blossoms on a spray of phalaenopsis orchids unfurl, from the lowest bloom to the topmost. Working with silk flowers teaches you to look for those details that make fresh flowers look real.

When you begin to look at flowers, observe their life cycle, how they look as young buds, and then, as their cycle evolves, notice how the buds unfold gradually, open to their fullest, and finally drop their petals. Now, put your observations to work. Create a glorious bouquet, then over time adjust the bouquet to re-create the different stages of its life cycle. Sculpt the flowers, gradually opening the buds, bending them at the stem. And finally, as they grow heavy with the weight of full bloom, cut a few petals off, letting them lie beneath the arrangement as they would in a fresh flower bouquet. There is a grace not only in the visual effect of following nature's patterns, but also in your participation in the process.

OPPOSITE: A bouquet reshaped to reflect the life cycle of the parrot tulip. At first the blossoms are tightly closed (top), then open (bottom), their stems bending to the light.

BELOW: Fading, the petals begin to fall.

FLOWER COLOR

*I*f you love flowers, then color is one of your passions—pastel pinks and vivid crimsons, blues in cool moonlight and deep sapphires, rich pumpkins and strawflower yellows. Color choices are critical to a successful arrangement. Here are a few guidelines to follow when you make your selections.

A color scheme imitating a swath of flowers growing in nature makes an arrangement easy on the eye. Therefore, some of the best designs use only one type of flower: a posy of violets or a stand of regal iris. Blending shades of one color is simply beautiful. For example, an arrangement of roses in tones of pinks or a simple summer bouquet of delphiniums in blues and purples looks natural.

Limiting color selection does not mean limiting the personality of the bouquet. Different sizes and shapes in the flower heads, from buds to open blossoms, or, as in the case of sunflowers, from smaller bloom heads to larger ones, provide dimension, so the arrangements never look boring. For still more variety, you can add preserved foliage or natural elements, which brings texture to the arrangement. A classical bouquet using a

OPPOSITE:
Stems seem freshly picked in this monochromatic blend of colors.

ABOVE:
Yellow blooms of cymbidium orchids and preserved foliage. The palm fronds mimic the shape of the container.

BELOW:
Avoid using a hodge-
podge of shapes and
colors in the same
bouquet.

OPPOSITE:
Variety is achieved in
a monochromatic
arrangement by
mixing different-size
flowers with
preserved foliage.

few of the same flowers is stunning. The most sophisticated arrangements are often the simplest, without embellishment or artifice.

You can also think about your choice of flowers in terms of seasonal arrangements. Certain colors bring to mind specific seasons. The strong color contrasts of spring may feel out of place as the year progresses. If you have the option of storing arrangements, you may decide to bring out another, more seasonally appropriate bouquet. If you plan to display one arrangement for several seasons, then more neutral colors of whites and creams or pale shades of any color make better choices.

To start planning your arrangement, evaluate the colors in the location where the arrangement will be placed. Flowers are an ideal decorative element. Their colors can be used as a transition to visually pull a space together, coordinating the tones in a couch, painting, or rug. Decide if you want the flowers to blend into your decor or to have strong color accents that add flair and drama. One strategy that always works to brighten a room is to place white blooms with greenery wherever you want to bring a sense of crisp light. Next time you go to buy flowers you may wish to bring a swatch of your upholstery fabric, or a pillow, in the shades you'd like to match. Narrowing down your options may help you avoid being overwhelmed by all the wonderful choices in the store. Just remember, fresh flowers are usually bought from the heart, not from a fabric sample. So if you fall in love with a color or flower that does not coordinate with your decor, make sure you use it to create a very natural-looking bouquet.

Beware the sometimes irresistible desire to include a whole rainbow of colors and variety of shapes in one bouquet. Arrangements with many differently colored blossoms may become overwhelming after a period of time. Incorporating too many different flower shapes often makes the arrangement look awkward and imbalanced.

The key to working with multicolored bouquets is to group similar colors together in masses, using white flowers or green foliage to separate the different blocks of colors.

An informal bouquet can handle a casual flower-bed mixture of many colors, while a more formal arrangement succeeds with a monochromatic arrangement of shades of just one color. Experiment with both styles, but when you are starting, the success of the simpler one-color bouquets will make you feel more confident.

To coordinate colors, select several flowers in your desired color range and hold them up to the natural light. Turn the flowers to see if the colors balance and blend together, or if they seem to fight one another.

There is a myriad of delicate details woven into a flower that can link colors to one another. Look for green shadings at the base of the flower where it joins the stem, or striations on the petals, which connect the eye to similar colors in other flowers. The bright dots of yellow pistils can be picked up in combination with yellow blossoms.

Restraining colors in a bouquet rarely limits your selection of flowers. When you choose white for an arrangement, you will be amazed at the subtle shadings of flowers, from snow white to buttermilk creamy white to beach sand white. Using various tones of the same color gives depth to an arrangement. A single color may also have undertones such as pink, green, or blue.

The flowers featured on the following pages illustrate the wide selection of color nuance, shape, size, and detail available within a single color. They are not necessarily flowers to be used together in a single arrangement, but they give you an idea of how many variations on a color can be found within each season. Study the photographs for ideas on which flowers may work best for your next arrangement.

OPPOSITE:
Neutral colors of white and green tone down and separate the contrasting colors in this bouquet of zinnias.

ABOVE LEFT:
The red-flecked center petals establish a relationship and coordinate the three contrasting colors of these peonies.

ABOVE RIGHT:
Selecting flowers in various shades of one color will give a monochromatic arrangement depth.

The Natural Approach to Design

Whites

CLOCKWISE FROM TOP LEFT:
Madonna lily (summer),
hyacinth (spring), cosmos
(summer), and rose (summer)
OPPOSITE: Calla lilies (summer)

Reds

CLOCKWISE FROM TOP LEFT: Gerbera daisy (summer and fall), peony (summer), Iceland poppy (summer), and protea (fall)
OPPOSITE: Ranunculus (spring)

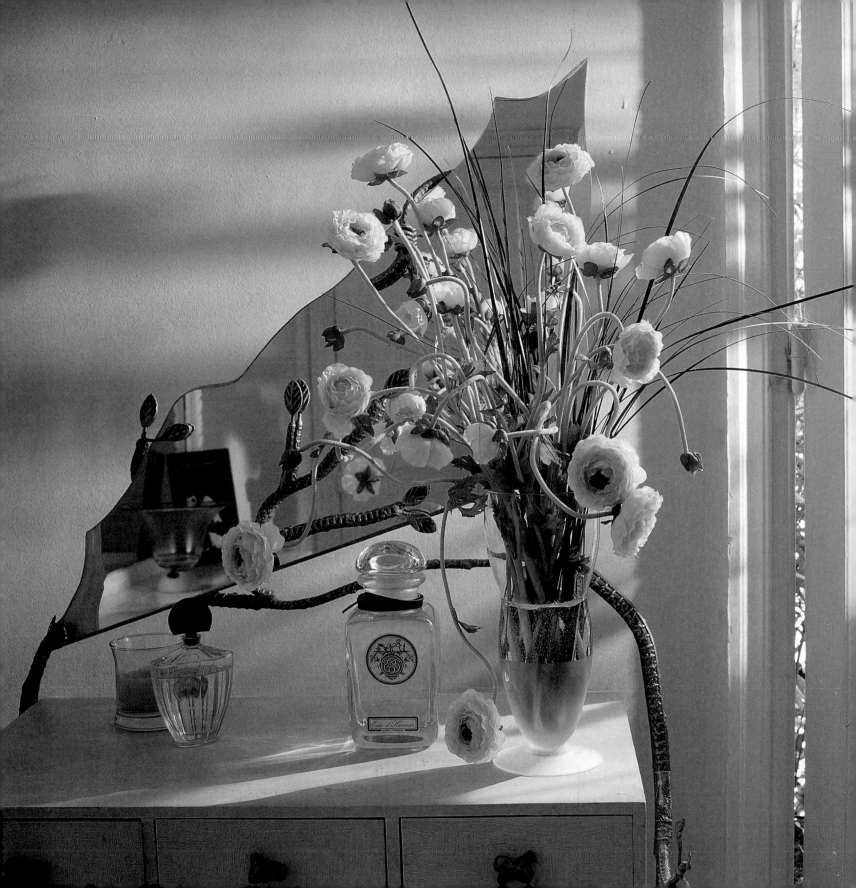

Yellows

CLOCKWISE FROM TOP LEFT:
Tiger lily (summer),
alstroemeria (summer),
sunflower (summer),
and bearded iris (spring)
OPPOSITE: Ranunculus (spring)

Purples

CLOCKWISE FROM TOP LEFT:
Iris (spring), delphinium (summer),
agapanthus (summer),
and foxglove (spring)
OPPOSITE: Foxglove (spring)

PERSONAL STYLE

Whether we prefer romantic, sophisticated, spare, simple, or country rustic moods, we all have a general sense of what visually pleases us. We may not always be able to name it, but if we begin training ourselves to notice what we respond to most strongly and identify its characteristics, we're on the path to learning how to duplicate the effect. Doing this successfully is what allows us to express a mood or a sense of our own style. The styles we prefer give us a subconscious feeling of balance and excitement; when we see the designs we love, either in a store, in someone's home, or even in a painting, we feel an internal sense of pleasure and satisfaction.

Style expresses itself through many different elements; color, form, texture, and scale all play different parts in building an ultimate arrangement style. What pleases you is a very particular juxtaposition of those elements, and no one person, company, magazine, or decorator can dictate that to you. The more you know about what pleases you, the more authority you will have over how to make arrangements yourself. You can look through magazines, books, and in the natural world to find what you like. We're all susceptible to following trends and being intimidated by the "experts," but you can always pick and choose for yourself. There's no such thing as a wrong style if it's what you love. Over time, with practice, your particular style will develop and you will approach new arrangements with confidence and direction.

Study the pictures in this book, noting how the arrangements combine color, form, and texture, and try them for yourself. Again, the best way to create wonderful bouquets is to look to nature, the ultimate stylist, and to imitate its spontaneity.

Sweet peas add color to a garden planter at the end of the blooming season.

RIGHT:
Japanese camellia
flowers shaped as if
they had just been
brought in from
outdoors.

OPPOSITE:
Tulips look as if
the petals were just
about to drop,
enhancing their
naturalness.

Selecting the Location

Selecting the location of your arrangement should be your first step in planning the design because the site influences the arrangement's scale, color, and shape. Walk around your home and look for locations that might benefit from a splash of color or brightness. Don't forget to include your outdoor living areas. To integrate the arrangement into the selected location, ask yourself the following questions:

- What is the overall space available for the bouquet?

- Should the arrangement be low and horizontal, tall and vertical, balanced or asymmetrical?

- Will the arrangement be seen from the front, or from all sides, from below or above?

- Are there predominant colors in the surroundings that should be taken into consideration?

- What kind of container suits the space and the atmosphere?

- Will the arrangement relate to a picture, mirror, or accessories?

- Is there natural light in the room or is the room dark?

The space available for the bouquet determines the proportions of the arrangement. This also gives you insight into appropriately sized flowers, not only their individual height or width, but the dimensions of their blooms.

The dimension of the bouquet must be scaled to its location and adapted to the style of the room. If the bouquet is to sit on a formal dining table for display as well as a centerpiece while dining, then a low bouquet is called for so that diners can see one another over the top of the bouquet. It cannot be so wide as to crowd the place settings. However,

if the arrangement is to be removed during dinner, then you can create whatever proportions please you.

The angle from which you see the arrangement also imposes a specific placement of the flowers. A centerpiece for a table will be seen from all angles, while a design for the living room coffee table will be seen from all sides as well as from the top, looking down. If an arrangement is to be seen only from the front, the flowers can be centered, using foliage filler to balance the back of the arrangement; if it will be placed on a shelf or mantel, then the flowers must be placed with at least some of the heads facing downward so the blossoms can be seen from below.

Flower arrangements are truly a finishing touch. They bring movement, energy, and color to an area, before (left) and after (below).

Placing the Arrangement

Flowers reflected in a mirror present a picture of elegance, the duplication enhancing the arrangement. Because you see both the front and back, the bouquet must present equally well. Flowers in front of paintings can complement the colors or images in the painting, but they should be designed so they relate without obscuring the painting.

When possible, place arrangements where they will receive natural light. Silk flowers are most enhanced by natural light because the transparency of the fabric allows the light to illuminate the blossoms, so they almost seem to glow. Next to a window, the light becomes almost painterly, like a still life. As the light changes from morning to night, the colors subtly alter to present an ever-changing scene.

Don't forget that you can place fabric flowers outdoors temporarily when you are entertaining and for special occasions. Flowers in a hand-held bouquet or added to a container dress up an area that you might normally ignore. Because the flowers are made of fabric, they should not be left out permanently; rain, the evening dew, and sunlight can affect the color.

The relationship between container, flowers, and the setting are critical to the beauty and balance of any arrangement.

OPPOSITE:
The graceful placement of phalaenopsis orchids in a glass vase is echoed in the mirror.

TOP:
Madonna lilies were arranged as a hand-held bouquet and released into a vase without being bound with string.

LEFT:
An unorthodox combination of cosmos, pansies, and vegetables make up a refreshing kitchen bouquet.

The Natural Approach to Design

Flower selection can be guided by the surroundings and the container. Roses create the liaison between the painting and the motif on the vase.

Taking the time to make the best selection of fine-quality fabric flowers is well worth the effort. Not only is selection important from an aesthetic standpoint, but because silk flowers last, your decisions have more long-term impact. Over the years you'll be making additions and changes, rearranging the flowers and moving them to new containers.

Before you shop, prepare by selecting the specific location for the arrangement and (if you already have one) the container. By this point you should have a good idea of color, scale, and style of the arrangement. It may help you to start out by choosing one of the arrangements from this book to use as a model. This preparation will be invaluable in helping you focus your decision making when you're in the store and stimulated by all the possibilities.

To find the best-quality flowers available, visit local florists, gift shops, and craft stores, looking carefully at the caliber of the flowers they offer and comparing them from shop to shop. Don't be discouraged when you first see the flowers, probably in the flat shape necessary for shipping. They may be wrapped in clear cellophane or they may be just set stiffly in a sales display. This in no way reflects their beauty to come. Rigidly flattened for packing, they

This anemone bouquet captures the spontaneity of fresh flowers from the market.

Flowers are packed flat and rigid for shipping (top). The petals are then opened and later artfully shaped into their loose, natural forms.

are one-dimensional. Ask the shop owner if you may take one or two out of the cellophane to shape, so you can see what the flower will look like once it is formed.

Superior-quality silk flowers capture the spirit of nature. Look for flowers in nature's colors; shrill colors make your bouquets look fake. Examine the backs and fronts of the petals and the leaves, noticing the color work. The petals in the best-quality flowers show subtle gradations in color, just as flowers do in nature. Examine the texture of the leaves and stems, and note whether the bark, thorns, or branch structure imitates the real plant.

A simple well-shaped flower paired with the illusion of water makes a strong statement as an arrangement.

Fine-quality flowers have hidden wires in many of the petals, leaves, and stems, enabling you to bend them to their natural shape. Check the stems to see that the joining of the branches is in character and the stem itself has variations in color and texture. This is especially important if you are planning an arrangement using the illusion-of-water technique, where realistic stems are vital to the trompe l'oeil.

When you have a pleasing selection of blooms you think coordinate well together, separate them from the sales display. If possible, take them over to a window to make sure the colors blend well — fluorescent lights mask the true colors. Hold the flowers up to the window so you can judge the color with the natural light flowing through the petals.

You may discover you have picked up too many flowers and the result is not satisfying. If this happens, start by eliminating flower types one at a time until you achieve a pleasing balance between color, shape, and size. Don't be discouraged; if necessary start over again.

OPPOSITE AND ABOVE:
These beautiful pink
zinnias exemplify quality
workmanship, which can
be seen in the texture
and intricate details
on the backs and fronts
of the petals, buds,
and leaves.

PART TWO

—

The Art of

Arrangements

NATURAL
GUIDELINES

A few simple guidelines are all you need to begin designing natural arrangements. But why do we need guidelines to do something freely? Though all artistic efforts arise from an instinctive place, they are also governed by a few principles that allow us to translate those instincts into a usable form; we are translating one language into another. As I described earlier in my introduction, underlying nature there is an elaborate design. It's the balance of the two, guidelines and instincts, that ultimately determines the success of the outcome. Although books and articles dictate rules and formulas to make elaborate bouquets of complex structures and intricate color combinations, I prefer to arrange fabric flowers simply, with an artlessness that makes them appear to have just been carried in from the garden. Those beginning to work with silk flowers will be more creative if they have not been trained to slavishly follow rules. But the principles I offer here, I offer in the hope of giving you the tools to free yourself of guidelines.

- Buy the best-quality flowers you can afford, for quality, not quantity, creates the most effective and satisfying bouquet. Even just one or two flowers standing in a circle of preserved foliage and placed in the appropriate container make an elegant statement.

- Reflect the seasons. Keeping step with nature has a natural rightness. Our home can be a place where we celebrate the natural world, putting us more in tune with life.

- Color choices are exceedingly important for beautiful arrangements. Devise a simple color scheme with the flowers you love, keeping in mind the colors that will surround the bouquet.

- Arrangements using all the same type of flower but in different shades and in different stages of development, from bud to bloom, look the most natural.

- When you arrange a multicolored bouquet, begin with the white or lightest-colored flowers first, gradually adding stronger or darker colors.

- In a multicolored bouquet, use white or green to make transitions between the blocks of color.

- The most pleasing arrangements come from a limited selection of a few flower types.

- Unlike the elaborate bouquets—with complex structures and intricate color combinations—designed by professional florists, fashion your arrangements to look like flowers just carried in from the garden.

- Each flower should be shaped individually while you create the arrangement, sculpting as uniquely as nature does to reflect the movement of living plants.

- Hours after you have completed your bouquet, critique your arrangement with a fresh view; do not hesitate to remove flowers—starting with the strongest colors. Empty space can create depth, and removing a flower can completely change an arrangement.

Of course, if you are not satisfied with your results, do not hesitate to start all over again. Never be afraid to start again. Giving yourself the freedom to rearrange, you will find that you have benefited from the first round with a better understanding of what your original intentions were. All the best creations result from a process of decisions and revisions, developing your vision as you go. Like every other learning process, arranging flowers is a process of discovery requiring that you pay attention and allow yourself to focus and get into the flow of creation.

Hyacinth sprays
with bulbs,
captured in an
illusion of water

When you are ready to begin arranging, you must first twist and bend the flowers into their natural form. Making flowers lifelike requires a sensitivity to their natural forms. This is where your observation of nature comes into play, where the artist and sculptor in you emerges.

As in nature, each flower should look a little different. The most effective results—those that truly fool the eye—happen when the arranger sees each individual stem as a unique growing plant. Notice the flowers illustrated in this book and see how leaves and stems are variously twisted and bent; how some stems are flexed, while others are arched. Then try to fashion the effect shown here by yourself.

Each flower stem should be shaped while you are creating your arrangement. The location you identify for the flower will guide you in determining the movement you want to give it.

Choose flowers at different stages of maturity. Leave some buds tightly curled while opening others so they appear to have been touched by the sun. Start by gently bending the stems and straightening them again so that although straight, they are softened and natural-looking.

An arrangement can be designed to reflect the evolution of flowers in nature. The buds of this tree magnolia are just opening (right). Later the flowers can be reshaped to full maturity with petals, snipped away with a scissors, strewn on the table below (opposite).

The leaves can be turned, bent up or down, and the stems flexed and arched. To shape the leaves, place a leaf between your thumb and index finger, and with a stroking motion, quickly brush the leaf between your fingers from the stem out to the tip. This helps flatten the leaf and gives it a good natural shape. Remember there are no straight lines in nature.

Arranging the Flowers

Arranging flowers is like mounting a theater production. Your room is the theater, the vase the stage, and the elements used in your arrangement are the actors, some playing more important roles than others.

Whenever possible, the best place to arrange the bouquet is in the location where you plan to place it. You can adjust the proportions as you work, making sure that it fits harmoniously into the space. Of course, there are some situations when it is not feasible

to arrange the flowers at their site. In this case, try to work on a pedestal or a tall counter that brings the arrangement up to waist level.

After fitting the container with foam, first place the flower that will be the farthest away from you. The space between this flower and you defines the area in which you will create your arrangement.

Remember to shape your flowers one stem at a time while creating the arrangement. Looking at your container, take the time to shape the flower for its specific location within the arrangement. If the petals are frayed, use embroidery scissors to trim off the threads. Professional florists carefully singe the edges with the flame of a candle to make the threads melt, but if you try this, be careful not to damage the flower.

Next, determine the height of the arrangement, pushing the tallest flower all the way down into the foam block. If you are using dramatic natural materials or preserved foliage as the tallest elements, begin with them. Next, place the flowers that mark the outer edges of your arrangement. These flowers constitute the foundation of the arrangement.

Once the basic foundation has been defined, cover the foam block with preserved foliage, filler flowers, or natural elements if necessary.

And finally add your principal players—the flowers that have the most personality, that play the most spectacular role. Hold the flower up to the container as if it were permanently placed. Simply bend the stem to calculate the length. When you are sure of the proper proportions, you can cut the stems.

If you decide you need more length, you can always reposition a slightly too-short stem in the foam block by simply pushing it in just enough to hold firmly, but not all the way down to the bottom.

If you find you've cut a stem too short, and you would prefer it longer, use a glue gun to glue the stem and its cut portion back together again by simply overlapping the

stem and gluing the two pieces back together. The glued portion won't show when the stem is pushed down into the foam block. Alternatively, you can use florist's tape, wound tightly around the overlapping stems. This tape, when stretched, becomes sticky, adhering to itself to make a good bond.

This hand-held bouquet of alstroemeria and ranunculus illustrates how balance can be achieved using preserved foliage, front view (left) and back view (right).

Always take the time to stand back and consider each addition and to observe the overall effect as you work. Turn the arrangement around. Regardless of how the arrangement is to be viewed, don't forget to balance the back with additional flowers, filler, or preserved foliage.

When you finish an arrangement, walk away. Come back when your mind is fresh to critique it and make the final adjustments. The challenge to creating natural-looking bouquets is to overcome the constraints imposed by the container. Now is the time to adjust your flowers slightly to push the limits of balance and proportion. Don't be surprised if you find yourself removing flowers to create more depth.

TECHNIQUES OF ARRANGING

The techniques that follow illustrate the three basic methods of arranging silk flowers: the illusion of water, hand-held bouquets, and florist's foam block arrangements. These examples are meant as guidelines that can be adapted to your containers and flowers. The detailed directions provide you with basic arranging skills to help you learn exactly how to create your designs with your materials. When you have mastered these techniques, you can prepare any of the arrangements in this book. A complete listing of all the arrangements and their elements will be found on page 125.

The Illusion of Water

Wild iris display

Here is the newest and most exciting development in silk flower arrangements: clear resin. The perfect partner for the new generation of silk flowers, clear resin presents the illusion of water so convincingly that it appears as though the cut flowers or bulbs were actually standing in water. Today's silk flowers have stems that are so accurately portrayed, they no longer have to be hidden away, as they were in the past. Not only do the stems of the flowers show up superbly in the clear glass vase, but bulbs, by themselves or teamed with natural elements such as moss, horsetail, beans, or pebbles, make for stunning presentations.

The simple process of mixing together two chemical compounds results in a liquid formula that when cured gives the appearance of clear water. Take care how you handle the chemicals by following all directions. To estimate the quantity of resin needed, before starting, pour water into your container up to the desired level, measure the quantity of water, and divide it by two to calculate the approximate amount of each chemical to use. Temperature affects the amount of time the resin takes to harden, but allow 18 to 24 hours.

You will need glass containers that hold liquid. The resin is permanent, so you cannot reuse the containers.

Hand-Held Bouquets

Of course, not every arrangement needs a container. Traditional hand-held bouquets are a classic French gift, so every florist has a selection to choose from. Hand-held bouquets of silk flowers offer great flexibility. They can be casually laid on a tabletop, so that they look freshly picked. Arrange them so that the stalks can support the bouquet standing up, or just slip them into a vase. Bulbs can be tied together with raffia, so that when clumped together, they stand upright. Look for objects that can be used for stands to support the flowers, either tied or in a tripod, giving the aura of a hand-held bouquet transfixed in space.

A bouquet of daffodils

Florist's Foam Block Arrangements

Floral designers use foam blocks hidden inside a container to hold fabric flowers permanently in position. Containers with narrow openings can hold flowers in a casual arrangement without foam, but generally, vases are filled with foam that is glued and wedged to create a firm foundation.

When you want to use a particularly beautiful clear glass or crystal vase with a large opening, glue only a small block of foam to the bottom, just enough to hold the flowers in the center of the container. Surround it with potpourri, Spanish moss, or rocks for a textured effect.

The two foam block arrangements shown here dramatically illustrate the variety of results you can obtain from the same basic steps. Using the same approaches but with different types of flowers, you can create dozens of beautiful arrangements for every season.

A delphinium garden

THE ILLUSION
OF WATER

Forcing Amaryllis

This simple arrangement in the illusion of water will give you a good introduction to the process, and the results will be dramatic!

Container

Amaryllis with bulb

Dried beans

Clear resin kit

A clean, disposable container, such as a
glass jar or unwaxed paper or plastic cup,
to mix the resin in

Stabilizing structure such as a wire frame from
an old lampshade or tripod of sticks

Mound moss

Tools: A clean stirring utensil,
entirely devoid of grease;
glue gun, wire, tape

Choose a container. A standard forcing vase that supports the bulb will make the arrangement simple and easy to complete.

Shape the roots, spreading the wiry strands out naturally. The flower can be shaped after the resin hardens.

Put beans into the bottom of the container. Place the bulb temporarily in the container to judge where the level of the resin should be. Mark the outside of the container with Scotch tape to indicate where the bottom of the bulb will be.

Mix the resin chemicals according to the package directions, making sure to follow all the precautions listed; protect your clothing, and try to prevent the resin from splashing on the edges of the container. Pour the resin into the container up to the Scotch tape mark. Immediately lower the bulb into the container. Attach the stem to the support with wire or tape to keep the bulb at the desired level.

Let the resin cure until it is completely hardened, 18 to 24 hours. Remove the Scotch tape and shape the flower. Glue or set the mound moss onto the top of the bulb.

Wild Iris Display

This is a weekend project, because the resin must be mixed and poured in two different stages with an interval of 12 to 18 hours. You must be able to leave the project undisturbed for 36 to 48 hours in an area with a room temperature of 60° to 80°F. Because temperature has an effect on how long it takes the resin to harden, there is no way to predict the exact amount of time required. As it hardens, the resin first turns rubbery, so you can test its consistency by touching the center of the resin carefully so as not to leave a permanent mark.

If you are short of time you can skip the first step—adding the horsetail to the bottom of the container. The arrangement will be equally dramatic with the bulbs alone.

Dried horsetail cut into pieces that fit into the container

Clear resin kit

2 white wild iris with bulbs (see *Note*)

4 yellow wild iris with bulbs

A clean, disposable container, such as a glass jar or unwaxed paper or plastic cup, to mix the resin in

Tools: A clean stirring utensil, entirely devoid of grease; scissors, a tripod of wooden dowels, wooden skewers, and string

Layer the cut horsetail pieces on the bottom of a clear glass container. Mix a small amount of resin according to the package directions, and pour the mixture over the horsetail. Use only as much resin in the first batch as needed to capture the horsetail in the bottom of the container. Let the mixture sit until it is just starting to solidify, 12 to 18 hours.

While the resin is hardening, prepare the tripod. Take three dowels and tie them with

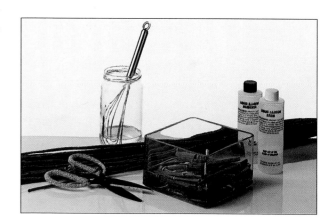

string in a teepee shape over the top of the container at a height that will allow you to suspend the flowers with the roots of the bulbs just touching the surface of the layer of resin. Suspend the flowers when the first poured resin has reached the rubbery stage.

Bend the stems in natural patterns and spread out the wiry roots. Suspend each flower from the top of the tripod with string or tape in the approximate position you desire for the arrangement. Then place the bulbs over the surface of the resin. If necessary, lay wooden skewers between the bulbs, extending over the edge of the vase, to stabilize your design. Use tape to fasten the skewers to the outside edge of the container.

Mix the remaining resin according to the package directions and pour it into the container, making sure the resin doesn't splash on the container wall or on the flowers. Let the resin cure until thoroughly hardened, an additional 18 to 24 hours.

When the resin is completely hard, remove the tripod and any skewers or tape used to stabilize the arrangement. Adjust and shape the flowers to complete the arrangement.

Note: Many bulbs come with a long metal pick that extends down four inches from the bulb. This is designed for use with a foam block, so when you are using a bulb in resin, you must use wire clippers to cut off the pick.

Sculptural Agapanthus

In France, chicken wire was traditionally used as a structural base to hold fresh flowers in place, serving the same function as flower frogs or florist's foam blocks do today. In this arrangement, the chicken wire replaces the tripod, holding the flowers steady until the resin dries; it also serves as an interesting sculptural element in the arrangement.

Chicken wire

6 agapanthus flowers

3 to 5 agapanthus leaves

Clear resin kit

A clean, disposable container, such as a glass jar or unwaxed
paper or plastic cup, to mix the resin in

Tools: A clean stirring utensil, entirely devoid of grease;
wire clippers

Cut a piece of chicken wire larger than the container. Fold it in such a way that it fills the inside of the container, touching the bottom. Unfold and shape the wire above the vase for a sculptural effect.

Open up the flowers, separating the individual blooms naturally. Place each flower and leaf in the container by threading the stem through the chicken wire to hold it in place.

Mix the resin according to the package directions, making sure the resin doesn't splash on the container wall or the flowers. Let the resin cure until thoroughly hardened, 24 to 48 hours.

When the resin is hard, bend the stems one by one in a graceful way that expresses the movement you would like to achieve in the arrangement. Then step back to judge the overall effect. Continue in this way until you are satisfied with the balance of the arrangement.

In this illusion of water, the chicken wire holds the stems in position and also serves as a sculptural element in the arrangement.

Kitchen Canning

$\mathcal{H}$ere's an original and wonderfully attractive use for the illusion created with resin. Jars filled with preserved fruits and vegetables of summer make a permanent decorative element on your counters or open shelves.

Plastic fruits and vegetables

Traditional canning jars or decorative glass jars

Chicken wire

Clear resin kit

A clean, disposable container, such as a glass jar or unwaxed
paper or plastic cup, to mix the resin in

Tools: A clean stirring utensil, entirely devoid of grease;
wire clippers, tape

Arrange the fruits and vegetables in the canning jars decoratively. Wedge them tightly together so the arrangement doesn't move when you rotate the jar.

Since the fruit may float to the top when the resin is poured into the jar, use a circle of chicken wire to keep the fruit pressed down until the resin hardens. Cut a round piece of wire twice as large as the diameter of the opening of the canning jar. Bend the wire down, forcing it firmly on top of the fruit or vegetables in the jar. Bend the edges of the wire over the top of the jar to fix it in position. If necessary, secure the wire with tape on the outside edge.

Mix the resin ingredients according to the package directions and pour the mixture into the container, making sure the resin doesn't splash on the edges of the container. Pour the resin through the chicken wire just up to the bottom of the mesh. Do not let the wire become affixed to the hardened resin.

Let the resin cure until thoroughly hardened, 18 to 24 hours. Remove the tape and chicken wire and put the lid on the jar.

Massed Peonies

This multicolored bouquet succeeds because the different colors are massed in blocks. The neutral white separates the yellow mass from the pink, and the color scheme is held together by the red-flecked center petals seen in all the flowers.

4 yellow peonies

5 white peonies

6 pink peonies

Tools: Wire clippers, thin green florist's string

Decorative ribbon or raffia

First shape the flowers. Start by gently bending the stems and straightening them again so that although straight, they are softened and natural-looking. Shape the flower heads to make them look lifelike, with all heads turning straight up so they can be seen when they are set into the bouquet. The leaves will be shaped after all the flowers are tied together into the bouquet.

Select the three flowers you want to place in the middle of the bouquet. Hold them in your hand, making sure that the stems do not cross. Take the string and tie the three stems securely together, wrapping the string around the stems several times. Don't cut the string at this stage, as you will be adding more blossoms.

Holding the stems in one hand, give the bouquet a one-quarter turn. Add one flower of the color you are assembling, keeping the heads at the same level. Continuing to turn in the same direction, give the bouquet exactly a one-quarter turn again. Do not let the stems cross. Wrap the string several times around the bouquet again. Continue in this way, turning a one-quarter turn each time and adding blossoms to mass the colors until you have added all the flowers. Wrap the string securely around the entire bouquet five or six times and then tie off and cut. If you wish, the string can be hidden with ribbon, raffia, or decorative cord.

Trim the stems to the desired length. Shape your silk flower bouquet, opening up some of the blossoms and bending the stems and heads so the bouquet looks natural. Fluff out the leaves.

A Bouquet of Daffodils

This freestanding daffodil bouquet sits upright, with the bulbs and moss as a base.

6 daffodils with bulbs (see *Note*)

Preserved foliage

Florist's wire

Raffia

Mound moss

Glue gun

Select the bulbs and preserved foliage for the center of the bouquet. Hold them in your hand. Take the wire and tie the stems securely together, then wrap the wire around the stems several times. Since this bouquet is quite large you may need to have someone else wrap the wire around the stems while you hold them with both hands.

Add the other flowers and preserved foliage, keeping the bulbs at the same level for a stable base. Wrap the wire several times around the bouquet again.

Shape your silk flower bouquet, bending the stems and heads so the bouquet looks natural. Fluff out the leaves and adjust the bulbs so the bouquet sits upright.

Tie the bouquet with raffia to disguise the wire binding. Then, using a glue gun, glue tufts of mound moss between the bulbs.

Note: Bulbs often come with a wire pick at the base that must be cut off with wire clippers for this hand-held bouquet.

FLORIST'S FOAM BLOCK ARRANGEMENTS

A Delphinium Garden

*A*lthough the directions may appear extensively detailed, this is a simple and quite beautiful arrangement.

2 florist's foam blocks

Container

Sheet moss (preserved foliage)

Florist's wire or black hairpins

10 delphinium stems

Tools: Glue gun, knife, wire clippers

First sculpt the foam block to fit the container, cutting away gradually with a knife until the foam fits inside the rim of the container. Once you have achieved a good fit, glue the block to the container. If you have used two or more blocks, or have used a number of wedges, first glue as many pieces together as you can while still fitting the block into the container. This step is very important because the foam is the foundation of your arrangement.

Cover the foam with pieces of sheet moss. Use wire shaped like a hairpin to secure the moss to the foam. Space the pins about every three inches. If you wish, you can trim the moss at the edge of the container or you can tuck it just inside the rim.

To create the structure for the arrangement, start with the tallest flower in your design. To determine its height, measure the stem of the flower by holding it next to the container. You can bend the stem for an accurate measurement of the height you desire. When you are sure of the height, cut the stem. If the stem is thick, as in the case of delphiniums, use heavy wire cutters to slice through the wire. If you have difficulty severing the wire, cut from both sides with wire clippers; when you bend the wire again, it should break.

Firmly push the stem through the moss into the foam block, pushing the stem all the way down to the bottom. If you do not like the placement, you can try a different location, but avoid making unnecessary holes or you'll have to begin again with new block.

Shape the flowers one at a time as you decide where to place them in the arrangement by gently bending the stems and straightening them again so that, although straight, they are softened and natural looking. Straighten the individual flowers so that the blossoms emerge directly from the main stem. Flatten out the leaves and bend them naturally.

Place the other key flowers, setting the boundaries of the design from back to front, and from side to side. Fill in the final flowers, taking time to walk around the arrangement or to step back and view it from a distance, with each additional flower. Once the flowers are in place, you can adjust them while holding the stems securely with the other hand to prevent them from being pulled out of the foam block.

Passionflower Arrangement

*A*llowing a single stem to star in an arrangement heightens its beauty. When selecting additional elements, choose those that harmonize in color or form, but that won't compete with the central flower.

Florist's foam block

Container

Woodland potpourri of small pinecones,
seedpods, and lichens

1 passionflower stem with 2 or more blooms

Horsetails

Mound moss

Florist's wire or black hairpins

Tools: Knife, wire clippers

With a knife, trim a piece of foam block just large enough to hold the passionflower stem and the horsetail. Glue down the block at the back of the container, leaving room to fill the sides with a woodland potpourri of small pinecones, seedpods, and lichens. Besides cleverly hiding the foam, the potpourri adds a subtle fragrance.

Place the stem into the foam block. Then firmly push in the dried horsetails, starting from the tallest and working down to the shortest. After placing them, you can trim off the tops to create a more pleasing design.

Finally, add the mound moss to hide the top of the foam block. You should not have to fasten the moss, but if you wish to, use folded wire or hairpins to fasten it down to the block.

A Suspended Rose Heart

*A*lthough this suspended heart uses just one color of petals, you can experiment with leftover petals of different shades from different flowers.

2 florist's foam blocks

Roses or rose petals

Nylon fishing line

Wire or black hairpin

Metal frame

Tools: Glue gun, knife, wire clippers, scissors

Glue the two foam blocks together securely. With a knife, carve the blocks into a three-dimensional heart shape, trimming just a bit off at a time until you reach the desired shape. If you wish, before you start, trace a rough outline of a heart on the foam block to guide your carving. Because you will be covering the foam with petals, the shape need only represent the general shape of a heart.

Pull the head of the rose off the stem. The pistil will come off easily and the rose petals can simply be pulled apart. With scissors, cut the groups of petals into individual pieces, neatly trimming the cut ends.

Starting at the bottom of the heart, use the glue gun to affix the first layer of petals all around the bottom point. Work your way up the heart by overlapping the petals, completely covering the foam from front to back. To make a natural-looking heart, offset the petals randomly as you work.

Measure enough fishing line to make a loop that will suspend the heart inside the metal frame. String the fishing line through a hairpin and push it down into the top of the heart, taking care that one of the petals covers the hairpin. Suspend the heart from the metal frame by tying the line around the frame, hiding the knot behind the frame.

PART THREE

—

The Seasonal

Approach

SAVORING THE SEASONS

*A*lthough we carry daybooks, enjoy monthly calendars with gorgeous full-color pictures of the things we love, or use computers to measure out the days, weeks, and years, in truth, most of us mark our lives by the seasons. Savoring the flowers of spring, with their evocative vibrant colors and textures, or the paper-thin crimped petals of summer poppies, or leathery grape leaves turning russet and gold in the fall, anchors our lives and gives us a firm base in the shifting and ceaseless flow of time. Our homes should reflect the seasons, celebrating change and possibility. Time your flower selections with these natural rhythms. Keeping your floral arrangements consistent with the time of year lends a vital, dynamic atmosphere to your home.

The first crocus heralding spring, drifts of yellow daffodils, the delicate ballet of tulip stems swinging in search of the light, the snow of apple blossoms drifting in a breeze—these flowers mark the arrival of spring after the long, dreary days of winter. Then tall sunflowers arch over plate-sized dahlias, whose blooms signal summer in neon blasts. With its heavy fragrance of spicy-sweet roses and the sizzling colors of zinnias, summer is replete with the bright polka-dot bursts of daisies and asters. Chrysanthemums and brightly colored fall leaves usher in autumn with its shortening days and nippy nights. Winter glistens with rose hips and holiday poinsettias. The exotic hothouse flowers of winter, orchids, stephanotis, and flowering ginger, add color to a snowy season quite bereft of flowers. Bulbs that are forced in winter to hurry up spring, such as hyacinth, crocus, and amaryllis, look wonderful suspended in the illusion of water.

Express the joy of gardening with a silk summer flower and herb bouquet lying in a traditional cutting basket.

Spring

Bundles of bulbs, blooming joyously, remind us that the world has again woken up from the long, cold, dark hibernation of winter. After the dull days of whites and grays, we rejoice to see wildly colorful mixtures of yellow and purple crocuses, red, white, and blue anemones, graceful irises in blues and whites, and of course, bushels of yellow daffodils, all blooming with cheerful abandon. Splash colors together in the spring in mixed bouquets of bright flowers, and put them in casual containers. Make elegant statements with the graceful swirl of tulip stems. Experiment with the stately soaring wild iris, subtly counterpointed with preserved foliage. Spring colors wake us up after the long, sleepy winter.

Pink, red, and white parrot tulips seem to dance as they arch and bend. Notice how the colors are massed and separated with white.

A display of spring daffodils and paper whites, immersed as though in clear rainwater, makes the spirit sing.

RIGHT:
Potted wild yellow,
pink, and white
lewisias stretch out of
their container, their
stems naturally
bending toward the
light. Ivy with deep
black berries fills
in the base.

OPPOSITE:
Yellow freesias,
splendidly displayed
with preserved
foliage, add interest,
texture, and
movement to a simple
arrangement.

ABOVE:
Tussie-mussies in clear resin
with violets and ivy

RIGHT:
Pips of lily of the valley emerge
from the mossy undergrowth.
Bits of moss add texture to the
sides of the container.

OPPOSITE:
Daffodils emerge from a mossy
cradle. Bear grass strengthens the
illusion of a patch of natural
meadow suddenly found
inside a room.

Summer

Summer heat is cooled down with the use of monochromatic palettes. Green foliage with accents of white flowers makes arrangements that appear cool and restful. Summer has glorious flowers in brilliant shades; revel in them, but limit your color range and add green to lighten the impact of the brighter shades. If your arrangement uses tones of colors, remember to mass each shade and use white to separate the color blocks. Summer celebrates the generosity of nature, so enjoy making large and glorious bouquets, using natural elements and preserved foliage to give lightness and texture to the arrangements. Summer is splendid and colorful, which makes the melancholy of its waning days all the more poignant—too soon the long, lingering days begin to shorten.

A small container balances this gangly mass of bright sunflowers, arranged from bud to full bloom. Moss spilling over the top makes the pot look as if it has just been brought inside.

Silk flowers added to planted urns
create dramatic focal points for an
outdoor event. Bearded irises
(opposite) look classic;
delphiniums (above) add grace.

Create the setting for
a memorable afternoon
tea with a hand-held
bouquet of roses.

Flowers can be arranged in
infinite ways. Here are three
different approaches to
arranging magnolias.

Three different approaches to arranging roses (from left): tea rose hand-held bouquet, roses with raspberry stems, and large open roses

Autumn
& Winter

As summer days begin to shorten and the harvest arrives, the seasons change once again. Fall leaves swirl around us in neon-bright colors, reflecting the last brilliant days before the world turns brown and later silvery with winter's icy touch. Gone are the soft-petaled, delicate flowers of spring and summer, but now there are wonderful conifers and exotic hothouse flowers such as blooming orchids. Here too are the earliest bulbs, tricked — some say forced — into glorious bloom by the warmth of the indoors. Even though snow may fall outside, flowers can still comfort us in our homes.

Phalaenopsia bloom in winter, but these carefree silk flowers paired with preserved foliage remain in bloom all year long.

RIGHT:

A hanging terra-cotta
container of
flowering stephanotis

FAR RIGHT:

A hanging container
holds pine,
pomegranates, and rose
hips with a graceful fall
of amaranthus, all bedded
with mound moss.
Combining unusual
textures and shapes
makes for an intriguing
arrangement.

OPPOSITE:

Stunning arrangements
need not be limited to
flowers. Try combining
grapes, sheet moss, and
raspberries for a fall
season arrangement.

ABOVE:

Lady's slipper orchids with mound moss, heather, and a bundle of tied horsetails make a miniature landscape, combining textures on different planes.

RIGHT:

An epidendrum orchid in a terra-cotta pot is set into a square glass container with clear resin as if the pot were being watered.

OPPOSITE:

Forced crocuses and moss in this shapely bell jar make a miniature world and cheer away winter blahs.

OPPOSITE:
Open roses and Queen
Elizabeth rose hips
intertwine on a grapevine
wreath. The loose form of
the rose vine contrasts with
the symmetrical shape and
texture of the wreath.

RIGHT:
A mixed fruit centerpiece
created on a bed of
eucalyptus

BELOW:
A harvest bouquet of
pomegranates, pears,
apples, and figs

PART FOUR

—

Tools and Materials

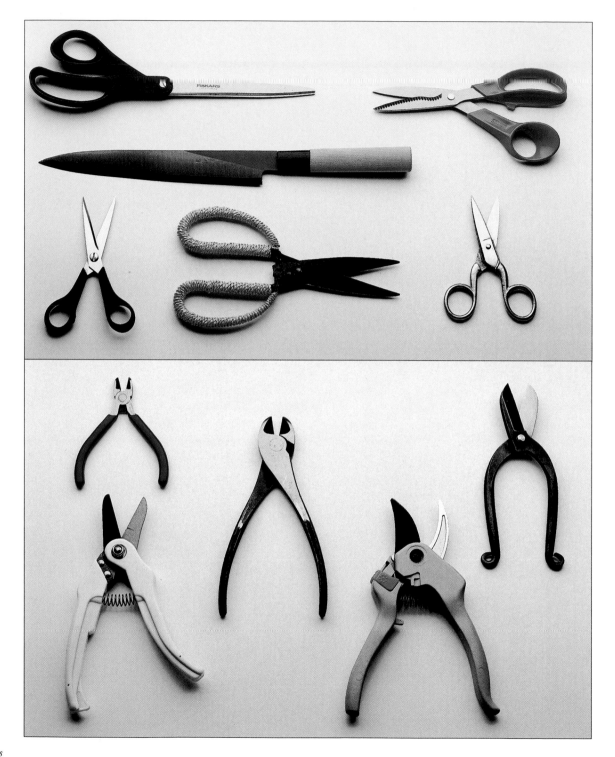

Choose scissors or light clippers to cut string and thin wires, but have one pair of strong clippers on hand for heavier wire stems.

*F*lower arranging needs your full concentration, so having the necessary tools and supplies handy clears the stage for the work itself. The tools are ordinary; you probably already have many of them in your home. But if you don't have these supplies, consider purchasing them because they make the mechanics of arranging flowers so much easier. Gather them up beforehand so they will be within reach.

The Basic Tool Kit

In your tool kit you'll need a sharp pair of clippers, either wire clippers or garden shears. Many arrangers prefer using wire clippers because the heavier wire in thick-stemmed flowers may be difficult to cut with the blades of garden shears. If you have problems cutting the wire with garden shears, try cutting around the stem, then bending the stem at the cut. It should snap off; if it doesn't, repeat the process.

A sharp knife is used to shape the foam block, trimming it to size for the container. Scissors or garden shears clip twigs or dried plant material.

Glue Guns

Glue guns release a thin stream of hot glue to attach moss, repair flowers, affix stems to florist's foam, or secure decorative elements. There are low-heat or high-heat guns. Make sure to buy the correct glue sticks for your gun; different guns use glue in a variety of diameters. A stick of glue melts inside the gun. With just a squeeze of the trigger, a drop of hot liquid glue is released precisely at the point where you aim it. The glue dries within 20 to 30 seconds. The amount of glue is regulated by the trigger.

Use caution when working with glue guns. Protect surfaces from excess drips when the gun is resting. Regardless of whether your gun is low-heat or high-heat, the tip of the gun or the hot glue can become hot enough to burn your skin severely.

Glue Pots

A glue pot allows a stick to melt into hot liquid glue that sits in an open pot. This type of dispenser makes it simple to dip in stems before affixing.

Glue guns, glue pots, and glue sticks are handy for a wide range of uses— not only for silk flower arranging— in every home.

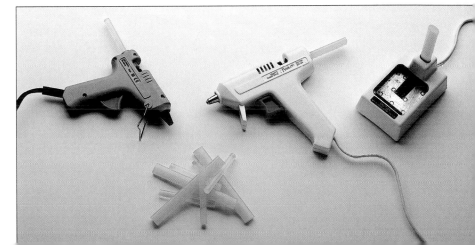

Florist's Foam Block

The dry florist's foam block is specifically designed for use with fabric flowers—unlike the wet block, which absorbs water for fresh-cut flowers. Because it can be a messy process, trim and fit the foam to the container in a different location from your work site. The trimming produces static crumbles, so cut the foam on top of a piece of newspaper, which you can wrap up and discard when finished.

Take your time when trimming the block, shaving off thin slivers of foam until it fits the form of the container. When you have completed fitting the block, the foam should be glued firmly to the base of the container using a glue gun, so it doesn't wiggle or move. If you are concerned about putting glue directly on the container, apply a piece of tape, such as duct tape, to the bottom of the container. Place the glue on the tape and then affix the foam. You can also use the smaller trim pieces to wedge the corners to assure that the block fits firmly into the container, keeping the finished arrangement stable.

For containers with narrow openings and sloping sides, you can only insert and glue a small piece of foam in the center of the container's bottom.

If the gun reaches down into the container, you can set beads of glue along the container's bottom, then fit the foam block on top of the glue. You can also apply glue to the bottom of the block and then set it in the container. If your container is glass, cover the piece of foam with moss, glass beads, potpourri, or other decorative elements.

The most important step before starting an arrangement is to make sure your block is fastened securely to the container. If the block seems loose, even after wedging and gluing, many professionals simply start over.

Florist's Wire

You can purchase florist's wire from a florist's supply or craft store. It comes both in straight lengths or on a metal bobbin. It is flexible and easy to use. When purchased, the wire is dark green, but it becomes almost invisible in arrangements.

Florist's Tape

Florist's tape comes in rolls in shades of green and brown. When you stretch the tape, it becomes sticky, clinging to a variety of surfaces. Florist's tape is great to use if your cut was shorter than you needed and you want to bind the stems back together.

Chicken Wire

Most hardware stores sell chicken wire by the foot, so you can buy small or large portions for your projects. Metal clippers cut through the wire easily, but use gloves because the wire can cut your hands.

Double-Stick Tape

Double-stick tape is sticky on both sides, allowing you to cover surfaces easily. You can create a mosaic of petals by applying tape to the surface of a plain container and transform it into something extraordinary by applying petals, leaves, moss, or other elements to the sticky surface. Cutouts of tape in any geometric shape can be shingled with natural elements to create a unique vase for an arrangement or a gift container.

Dust Removers

A small can of compressed air is a good way to thoroughly dust flowers. Follow the directions on the container. A feather duster also works magic, displacing the dust without affecting the positioning of the flowers.

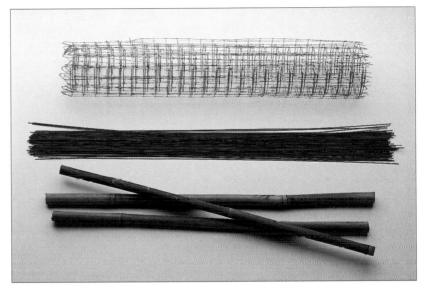

OPPOSITE:
Clockwise from top left:
Double-stick tape, florist's tape,
florist's string, and wire

ABOVE:
From top to bottom:
Chicken wire, precut florist's wire,
and bamboo poles

CONTAINERS

Often the container dictates the style of the bouquet. It's crucial that both flowers and container be in harmony with each other. Select containers that are easy to use and proportionate to the space the composition will occupy.

The color of the container, its finish, and its overall look should all be taken into account when selecting your flowers. A terra-cotta pot begs for an informal splash of flowers, while a crystal bowl wants a stately blend of elegant roses.

Leaky containers are never a problem with silk flowers. Because the flowers don't require water, you have infinite options. There are probably many containers around your home that can be used, even those that are cracked. Moss can be glued over deformities or flowers bent to hide the chips.

A Wrapped Container

Draping fabric around a vase allows you to use a pattern from your decor to coordinate with the vase. Cloth disguises tin cans, simple garden terra-cotta pots, or inexpensive containers that have a form you like.

Other Containers

Challenge yourself to think of new ways to cover containers with natural elements. Cover the container with moss, wrap it in straw, entwine it in sisal, or camouflage it with flower petals.

Natural elements in arrangements of fabric flowers add texture, color, and fragrance making them even more convincing. Bare branches or dried horsetails add bonelike architecture that contrasts with the soft, billowy petals of the flowers. By using upright elements you can create height with a strong vertical line. Adding fragrance to arrangements creates still another dimension.

Preserved Botanicals

Nearly everyone has seen carnation blossoms dyed exotic colors by placing the stems in a solution of dye. Using a similar method, plant manufacturers use the plants' ability to wick up moisture through their stems to absorb a preserving liquid. The key component of the liquid is glycerin, an organic compound of fats found in many food products. Some dye is added to the solution to help the plant retain its natural coloring, but it is water soluble. The results are marvelous: natural leaves and blossoms that are perfectly lifelike and supple, lasting for up to ten years. Some shop clerks may offer you a different kind of dried material when you request the preserved botanicals, so check to make sure they are preserved, because the difference is remarkable.

Using preserved botanicals with silk flowers makes an arrangement look more lifelike, because the preserved foliage is a natural product. Added as fill, the greens act as a neutral, setting off the floral colors to their best

Although most of the preserved botanicals are foliage plants such as (top to bottom) bear grass, horsetail, ivy, amaranthus, or silver dollar eucalyptus, there are also heathers with blossoms to accent arrangements.

advantage. Preserved foliage creates a natural setting for flowers. Their color, reality of texture, and fragrance underscore the lifelike quality of the arrangement. Filling out a bouquet using just one type of flower with preserved foliage provides form and interest while maintaining a simplicity of line. The contrast of preserved moss around the base of bulbs or at the bottom of a tall arrangement adds drama and texture.

On rare occasions, with conditions of high humidity, the pores of the preserved foliage may become unsealed, causing the solution to leak out in small drops from the plant's pores. This rarely occurs under normal conditions. Although the dyes are water soluble and usually wash out, make sure to place the arrangement on a surface that will not be damaged or stained.

Dried Materials

You can buy twigs and dried material from a florist or florist's supply shop or you can make your own. Hang the seed heads or plumes of summer grasses upside down in a paper bag in a dark closet or attic until they are stiff and thoroughly dried. Gather mossy twigs year round, or cut branches and let them dry out before using them. Make sure to have an adequate supply for each arrangement by drying more than you think you may need. That way, if your arrangement takes a new direction, you will always have enough materials on hand to satisfy your needs. Remember that the dried materials may not last as long as the silk flowers or preserved foliage, and if the seed heads shatter or the grasses begin to look tattered, you will need to redo the arrangement.

Find interesting objects to add to the resin. Materials added to the container displace the resin, so you need less liquid to fill it.

LEFT:
Stones

BELOW:
Dried beans

BOTTOM:
Glass beads

Natural Treasures

Polished rocks, dried beans or peas, or seashells can be used to cover the foam block, providing texture and color to the bottom of the arrangement. Many of these can be purchased, but don't hesitate to take a walk in the woods to gather small pinecones, pieces of bark, lichens, or chips of wood.

Adding treasures to the resin displaces the liquid; consequently, you need less of it to fill a container. However, make sure to wash and dry the objects carefully before adding them. Some rocks have a powdery surface that may cloud the resin.

Fragrance

If you miss the fragrance of fresh flowers, you can spray your silk flowers with one of the extensive choices of floral scents or essential oils now available. Make sure you choose one that blends with or complements the flowers in your design. Little packets of potpourri can also be hidden among the flowers of almost any arrangement. Or you can fasten a small foam block—just large enough to hold your flowers—to the center of the container, and then fill up the space with a fragrant potpourri. Cinnamon sticks lining a container conceal a foam block while subtly perfuming the room with clean, spicy sweetness. Since wood absorbs fragrant oil readily, wood chips, bark, or pinecones can soak up an essential oil to incorporate fragrance in your bouquet.

You can break off a stick of cinnamon periodically to release its fragrance to this arrangement of Dutch iris with bear grass and mound moss.

LIST OF INGREDIENTS FOR BOUQUETS

Page 2: Peony, asparagus fern Page 6: Ranunculus, phylica, bear grass Page 8: Bergamot, monk's hood, gypsophilia, heather, sheet moss, mound moss, lichen Page 12: Large open rose, large rosebud Page 18: Cosmos, tiger lily Page 20: Parrot tulip Page 22: Agapanthus, mini cornflower, mini iris Page 23: Cymbidium orchid, washingtonia leaves, bear grass, silver dollar eucalyptus, amaranthus Page 24: Bearded iris, Iceland poppy, rosebud, wild delphinium Page 25: Poppy anemone, ranunculus, ivy with berries Page 26: Zinnia; Page 27: (left) Peony; (right) poppy anemone Page 30: Ranunculus, bear grass Page 32: Ranunculus, bear grass Page 34: Foxglove, silver dollar eucalyptus Page 36: Sweet peas Page 38: Japanese camellia, ivy with berries Page 39: French tulip, French tulip bud Page 41: Iceland poppy, sheet moss Page 42: Phalaenopsis orchid, phalaenopsis leaf Page 43: (top) Madonna lily, red gum eucalyptus; (bottom) cosmos, pansy spray, loquats, peppers, pomegranate, ivy, broom, sheet moss Page 44: Full open tea rose, large open tea rose, tea rose bud Page 46: Poppy anemone Page 49: Lilium lily, bear grass Page 52: Iceland poppy Page 54: (clockwise from top left) Stephanotis, Phalaenopsis orchid, phalaenopsis leaf, cymbidium orchid, cymbidium leaf, wild crocus, sheet moss, amaranthus Page 57: Hyacinth spray with bulb, dried beans Page 60: Tree magnolia, pine, mound moss Page 61: Tree magnolia, pine, mound moss Page 63: (left) Alstroemeria, bittersweet, ranunculus, ivy, bear grass, heather; (right) alstroemeria, bittersweet, ranunculus, ivy, bear grass, heather Page 84: High bush cranberry, open rose Page 86: Astrantia, bergamot, borage, burnet, butterfly lavender, French lavender, sage, sunflower bud, yarrow, bear grass, sheet moss

Page 89: Parrot tulip, sheet moss Page 90: Wild daffodil, wild narcissus, paper white Page 92: Wild lewisia, ivy with berries Page 93: Freesia, freesia leaf, bear grass, gynerium Page 94: (above) Violets, ivy with berries; (below) lily of the valley, phylica, mound moss Page 95: Wild daffodil with bulb, bear grass, mound moss Page 97: Giant sunflower, sunflower bud, sheet moss Page 98: Bearded iris, bear grass, horsetail Page 99: Wild delphinium, ivy with berries, broom, sheet moss Page 100: Full open rose, large rosebud, Queen Elizabeth rose hips, rose leaves Page 102: Magnolia, pine, sheet moss Page 103: (left) Tree magnolia, ranunculus, kangaroo paw, phylica, ivy, bear grass; (right) magnolia, small magnolia, ivy with berries, bear grass Page 104: (left) Large open tea rose, tea rose bud, ivy; (right) American raspberry, full open rose, corkscrew willow Page 105: Large open rose, large rosebud, bear grass, ivy Page 107: Phalaenopsis orchid, phalaenopsis leaf, amaranthus, sheet moss Page 108: (left) Stephanotis, sheet moss; (right) pomegranate, pine, amaranthus, mound moss, Page 109: American raspberry, mini grape branch, sheet moss Page 110: (left) Lady's slipper orchid, bear grass, heather, horsetail, mound moss; (right) wild epidendrum, sheet moss, bear grass Page 111: Crocus, mound moss, river rocks Page 112: Large open rose, Queen Elizabeth rose hips, grapevine wreath Page 113: (left) Pomegranate, pear, apple, fig, sheet moss, pine, bear grass, phylica; (right) apple, pear, fig, plum, banana, cherry, grape, eucalyptus, ivy Page 120: Hyacinth spray, mound moss, ivy with berries, statice, asparagus Page 122: Cosmos, mini cornflower, wheat, bear grass Page 124: Iris, iris bud, bear grass, mound moss, cinnamon sticks

ACKNOWLEDGMENTS

Like an arrangement of flowers made from many individual stems, this book has been created with many people in my life. Mary Hardy inspired me to consider a book project and then assisted me in completing it.

I am grateful for the help of my agent, Elyse Cheney, of Sanford J. Greenburger Associates, Inc.; editor Gail Kinn of William Morrow; Mimi Luebbermann, who wrote the text; Régine de Regaini, who graciously invited us into her home; and Louis Gaillard for his exquisite photography. All helped to bring these bouquets to life. Joel Avirom, Meghan Day Healey, and Jason Snyder produced the elegant book design. My thanks to contributers Christopher Robba and Lucien Pietrois. Also thanks to Susan Nicholson of Ireko, Santa Rosa, for technical information. Thanks to the research staff, Pascal Beauvais, Moussa Dadda, and Sophie Leonetti, who helped gather the materials for the countless bouquets.

All of this would have been impossible without the staff of Emilio Robba. Thanks go to Dominique Allier, Katia Chaix, Ursula Dechant, Ewa Figuera, Nadia Gallardo, Sandrine Gimonet, Sylvie Gouilly, Renee Heinecke, Marie-Christine Lafosse, Philippe Lozano, Françoise Nicolas, Bruno Peutat, and Carole Siyahian.

And of course, my endless gratitude to my wife, Nicole, my brother Michel Robba, my sister Marie-Ange Loisy, and my friend Jean-Pierre de Regaini.

My appreciation goes to the Tai family, Patrick, Garrison, Edward, and Hans Juffermans, as well as the staff of Winward Silks, both in the day-to-day work of my business and also in their generosity in supplying the flowers for the bouquets and arrangements pictured in the photographs.

I would like to recognize my friend and business associate Mr. Kingo Tsujimura, whose clarity of vision has always been an inspiration to me, along with everyone at Itokin Co. Ltd. who works so diligently for Emilio Robba in Asia.

And finally to Alain de Saint-Sauveur, who was one of the first to believe in the Emilio Robba style.

SOURCES

UNITED STATES
Emilio Robba, 303 Cognewaugh Road, Greenwich-Cos Cob, CT 06807 Tel: 1-800-745-7656 Fax: 1-203-661-4419 or E-mail: info@robba.com

EUROPE
Emilio Robba, 29-33 Galerie Vivienne, 75002 Paris, France Tel: (33) 1 4261 7143 Fax: (33) 1 4261 3853

ASIA
Itokin Co. Ltd., Emilio Robba Division, 2-4-8, Bakuro-Machi, Chuo-Ku, Osaka, Japan Tel: (81 6) 263 6306 Fax: (81 6) 263 6308

Winward Silks:
International importer and distributor of fine-quality silk flowers
For your local distributor call: 1-800-888-8898
or E-mail: wsilks@winwardsilks.com
http://www.winwardsilks.com

Kits are available for many of the arrangements featured in this book. For information call: 1-800-888-8898

INDEX

Page numbers in **bold** refer
to illustrations.

agapanthus, **35**, 70–71
alstroemeria, **33**, 63
amaryllis, 66–67, 87
anemones, **47**, 89
arranging, 53–83
   natural guidelines for, 55–57
   process of, 60–63
   techniques of, 64–83; *see also* florist's
     foam block arrangements; hand-
     held bouquets; illusion of water
autumn arrangements, **31**, 87, 106–113

beans, 64, 67, 123, **123**
bear grass, **94**, **121**, **124**
bulbs, **57**, 64, 65, 67, 68, 69, 76, 87,
   107

camellias, **38**
Cardin, Pierre, 9
centerpieces, 40–41
chicken wire, 70, **71**, 72, 119, **119**
cinnamon sticks, 124, **124**
clippers, **116**, 117, 119
color selection, 23–35, 48, 49, 56, 107
   monochromatic, 23, **23**, **24**, 27, **27**,
     97
   purple, **34–35**, 89
   red, 30–31, 89, **89**
   white, 24, 27, **27**, **28–29**, 56, 89, **89**,
     92, 97
   yellow, **23**, 27, **32–33**, 89, **92**
containers, **23**, 43, 44, 62, 63, 64–65,
   66, 78, 80, 89, **94**, **97**, **108**, 118
   clear glass, 64, 65, **110**
   selection of, 40, 43, 120
   wrapped, 120
cosmos, 29, 43
crocuses, 87, 89, **110**

daffodils, 87, 89, **91**, **94**
   bouquet of, **65**, 76–77
daisies, **31**, 87
delphiniums, 23, **35**, **99**
   in delphinium garden arrangement,
     65, 78–79
double-stick tape, 119, **119**
dust removers, 119

essential oils, 124
eucalyptus, **113**, **121**

florist's foam block, 117, 118, 123, 124
florist's foam block arrangements, 11,
   62–63, 64, 65, 78–83, 118
   delphinium garden, **65**, 78–79
   passionflower, 80–81
   suspended rose heart, 82–83
florist's tape, 63, 119, **119**
florist's wire, 76, 78, 80, 118, **119**
foxglove, 35
fragrance, 121, 122, 124
freesias, 92
fruit, **108**, **113**

garden shears, 117
glass beads, 118, **123**
glue guns, 62, 76, 117, **117**, 118
glue pots, 117, **117**

hand-held bouquets, 11, 43, **43**, **63**, 64,
   65, 74–77, **87**, **100**, **104**, 120
   daffodils, **65**, 76–77
   massed peonies, 74–75
heathers, **110**, **121**
horsetails, 64, 68, 80, **110**, 121, **121**
hyacinths, **29**, **57**, 87

ikebana, 10
illusion of water, 11, 49, **49**, **57**, 64,
   66–73, 87, **91**, **110**

clear resin and, 64–65, 67, 68–69, 70,
   72, **94**, **110**, 123
   forcing amaryllis in, 66–67
   in kitchen canning, 72–73
   sculptural agapanthus in, 70–71
   wild iris display in, **64**, 68–69
irises, **33**, **35**, 89, **99**, **124**
   in wild iris display, **64**, 68–69
ivy, **92**, **94**, **121**

kitchen canning, 72–73

lewisias, 92
life cycle, 20–21, **21**, 56, 58, **58**, **60**
light, 13, **13**, 24, 27, 40, 43, 49
lilies, **29**, **33**, 43
lily of the valley, 94
location selection, 24, 40–41, 47, 60–62

magnolias, **17**, **58**, **60**, 103
massed peonies bouquet, 74–75
materials, 115–124
   see also containers; natural elements;
     specific materials
Mende-en-Gévaudan, Seguin de, 14
monochromatic palettes, 23, **23**, **24**, 27,
   27, 97
moss, 9, **9**, 64, 65, 67, 76, 80, **94**, **97**,
   108, **110**, 118, 122, **122**, **124**
Musée d'Histoire Naturelle, 9

natural approach, 19–51
   color selection in, *see* color selection
   flower selection in, 47–51, 55
   guidelines for, 55–57
   life cycle in, 20–21, **21**, 56, 58, **58**, **60**
   lifelike appearance in, 11, 58–61, 121,
     122
   location selection in, 24, 40–41, 47, 62
   personal style in, 37–45
   placement in, 11, 41, 42–45, **99**, 122

natural elements, **9**, 23, 62, 64, 97, 119, 120, 121–124
 see also preserved botanicals

orchids, **16**, **17**, **23**, **43**, 87, 107, **110**
outdoor placement, 11, 43, **99**

packing for shipment, 17, 47–49, **48**
pansies, **43**
passionflower arrangement, 80–81
pebbles, 64, 65, 123, **123**
peonies, **27**, **31**
 bouquet of, 74–75
personal style, 37–45
placement, 41, 42–45, 122
 outdoor, 11, 43, **99**
poppies, **11**, **31**, 86
potpourri, 65, 80, 118, 124
preserved botanicals, 121–122
 foliage, 23, **23**, **24**, 62, 63, **63**, 76, 78, 89, **92**, 97, **107**
 moss, 64, 65, 67, 76, 80, **94**, **97**, **108**, **110**, 118, 122, **122**, **124**
purple flowers, **34–35**, 89

raffia, 65, 74, 76, **120**
ranunculus, **31**, **33**, **63**
red flowers, **30–31**, 89, **89**
resin, clear, 64, 67, 68–69, 70, 72, **94**, **110**, 123
roses, 23, **29**, **44**, 87, **100**, **104**, **113**, 120
 in suspended rose heart, 82–83

scissors, **116**, 117
sculptural agapanthus arrangement, 70–71
seasonal arrangements, 11, 24, 55, 85–113
 autumn, **31**, 87, 106–113
 spring, **29**, **31**, **33**, **35**, 87, 88–95
 summer, 23, **29**, **31**, **33**, **35**, 87, **87**, 96–105
 winter, 106–113
silk flowers, 10–11, 13–17
 packing for shipment of, 17, 47–49, **48**
 selection of, 47–51
singeing, 62
spring arrangements, **29**, **31**, **33**, **35**, 87, 88–95

stephanotis, 87, **108**
summer arrangements, 23, **29**, **31**, **33**, **35**, 87, **87**, 96–105
sunflowers, **33**, 87, **97**
suspended rose heart arrangement, 82–83
sweet peas, **37**

tools, 116–117
tulips, **21**, **38**, 87, 89, **89**
tussie-mussies, **94**

vegetables, **43**, 72–73
violets, **94**

white flowers, 24, 27, **27**, **28–29**, 56, 89, **89**, **92**, 97
wild iris display, **64**, 68–69
winter arrangements, 106–113
wrapped containers, **120**

yellow flowers, 23, 27, **32–33**, 89, **92**

zinnias, **27**, **51**, 87